The Teacher Development Continuum in the United States and China
Summary of a Workshop

Ana Ferreras and Steve Olson, *Rapporteurs*
A. Ester Sztein, *Editor*

U.S. National Commission on Mathematics Instruction

Board on International Scientific Organizations

Policy and Global Affairs

NATIONAL RESEARCH COUNCIL
OF THE NATIONAL ACADEMIES

THE NATIONAL ACADEMIES PRESS
Washington, D.C.
www.nap.edu

THE NATIONAL ACADEMIES PRESS 500 Fifth Street, N.W. Washington, DC 20001

NOTICE: The project that is the subject of this report was approved by the Governing Board of the National Research Council, whose members are drawn from the councils of the National Academy of Sciences, the National Academy of Engineering, and the Institute of Medicine. The members of the committee responsible for the report were chosen for their special competences and with regard for appropriate balance.

This study was supported by the National Science Foundation under Grant No. 0638656. Any opinions, findings, conclusions, or recommendations expressed in this publication are those of the author(s) and do not necessarily reflect the views of the organizations or agencies that provided support for the project.

International Standard Book Number-13:   978-0-309-15163-4
International Standard Book Number-10:   0-309-15163-5

Additional copies of this report are available from the National Academies Press, 500 Fifth Street, N.W., Lockbox 285, Washington, DC 20055; (800) 624-6242 or (202) 334-3313 (in the Washington metropolitan area); Internet, http://www.nap.edu.

THE NATIONAL ACADEMIES
Advisers to the Nation on Science, Engineering, and Medicine

The **National Academy of Sciences** is a private, nonprofit, self-perpetuating society of distinguished scholars engaged in scientific and engineering research, dedicated to the furtherance of science and technology and to their use for the general welfare. Upon the authority of the charter granted to it by the Congress in 1863, the Academy has a mandate that requires it to advise the federal government on scientific and technical matters. Dr. Ralph J. Cicerone is president of the National Academy of Sciences.

The **National Academy of Engineering** was established in 1964, under the charter of the National Academy of Sciences, as a parallel organization of outstanding engineers. It is autonomous in its administration and in the selection of its members, sharing with the National Academy of Sciences the responsibility for advising the federal government. The National Academy of Engineering also sponsors engineering programs aimed at meeting national needs, encourages education and research, and recognizes the superior achievements of engineers. Dr. Charles M. Vest is president of the National Academy of Engineering.

The **Institute of Medicine** was established in 1970 by the National Academy of Sciences to secure the services of eminent members of appropriate professions in the examination of policy matters pertaining to the health of the public. The Institute acts under the responsibility given to the National Academy of Sciences by its congressional charter to be an adviser to the federal government and, upon its own initiative, to identify issues of medical care, research, and education. Dr. Harvey V. Fineberg is president of the Institute of Medicine.

The **National Research Council** was organized by the National Academy of Sciences in 1916 to associate the broad community of science and technology with the Academy's purposes of furthering knowledge and advising the federal government. Functioning in accordance with general policies determined by the Academy, the Council has become the principal operating agency of both the National Academy of Sciences and the National Academy of Engineering in providing services to the government, the public, and the scientific and engineering communities. The Council is administered jointly by both Academies and the Institute of Medicine. Dr. Ralph J. Cicerone and Dr. Charles M. Vest are chair and vice chair, respectively, of the National Research Council.

www.national-academies.org

Preface and Acknowledgments

In 1999, Liping Ma published her book *Knowing and Teaching Elementary Mathematics: Teachers' Understanding of Fundamental Mathematics in the United States and China*, which probed the kinds of knowledge that elementary school teachers need to convey mathematical concepts and procedures effectively to their students. Later that year, Roger Howe, a member of the U.S. National Commission on Mathematics Instruction (USNC/MI), reviewed the book for the *Notices of the American Mathematical Society*, concluding that it "has lessons for all educational policymakers." Ma's book caught the attention of many mathematicians and mathematics educators, sparking an interest in Chinese mathematics teaching that continues to this day.[1]

Several years ago, Professor Howe was attending an international conference on mathematics education when a particular phrase caught his ear; the Chinese educators often talked of "superrank" teachers, i.e. teachers with the honor of "Special Class" (*Te Ji Jiao Shi* in Chinese). This is an honorary designation in the Chinese career teacher hierarchy that involves special responsibilities for leadership, professional development, and research. Although there is no equivalent designation in the United States, the common roles of master teachers in both countries are math coaches

[1]National Research Council. 2003. Understanding Others, Educating Ourselves: Getting More from International Comparative Studies in Education. Colette Chabbott and Emerson J. Elliott, eds. Committee on a Framework and Long-term Research Agenda for International Comparative Education Studies.

and consultants, technology coordinators, mentor teachers, mentoring and induction coordinators, peer reviewers, special education inclusion coordinators, department chairs, grade-level team leaders, and house leaders.

Concluding that this was something U.S. educators wanted to know more about, Professor Howe shared this information with the USNC/MI.[2] Intrigued by the idea of superrank teachers, the USNC/MI sponsored a workshop entitled "The Teacher Development Continuum in the United States and China." The purpose of the workshop was to examine the structure of the mathematics teaching profession in the United States and China, as described in the following statement of task:

> A public workshop will be organized that will bring U.S. and Chinese experts on mathematics education together to discuss professional development methods and techniques commonly used in their countries. The workshop will feature invited presentations and discussion that will focus on the teacher development process used in the U.S. and China, and how the professional lives of teachers are structured to receive ongoing professional development. The activity will bring together U.S. and Chinese experienced and highly qualified teachers that provide professional development (such as master teachers, mentors, or coaches). Comparing and contrasting the roles and status of master teachers in both countries will be one of the main goals. An individually-authored workshop summary and a 13-minute video with highlights of the event can be found at http://sites.national academies.org/pga/biso/ICMI/.

Held in Newport Beach, California, on July 31–August 2, 2009, the workshop brought together about 40 mathematics educators, mathematicians, education researchers, and other mathematics education specialists from the two countries. There were participants from three regions of China, Beijing, Shanghai, and Jiangsu Province (north of Shanghai), as well as several Chinese scholars who now work in the United States. A graduate

---

[2]The USNC/MI plans, recommends, and encourages projects in areas of international importance in mathematics education and also advises the National Research Council on all matters pertaining to the International Commission on Mathematical Instruction. The International Commission on Mathematical Instruction is a commission of the International Mathematical Union, which is an international, nongovernmental scientific organization with the goal of promoting international cooperation in mathematics.

student at the University of California, Irvine, Xiaoqing Chen, provided superb translations, with assistance from several bilingual scholars among the Chinese and Chinese-American participants. The workshop was planned and organized by two staff members from the Board on International Scientific Organizations (Ana Ferreras and Kofi Kpikpitse), with the assistance of five USNC/MI members: Patrick (Rick) Scott, New Mexico Higher Education Department; Joseph G. Rosenstein, Rutgers University; Janine Remillard, University of Pennsylvania; Roger Howe, Yale University; and Ann Lawrence, Capitol Hill Day School (retired). We would also like to express thanks to Ester Sztein for editing this report. There was no official National Research Council (NRC) planning committee.

Workshop planners benefitted from information from a November 2008 meeting on "Building on Cross-National Comparisons to Improve the Preparation and Support of Teachers of Mathematics," organized by Janine Remillard under National Science Foundation (NSF) grant 0738019. This earlier meeting, together with the 2009 workshop, provided invaluable insights into the teaching of mathematics and the preparation of mathematics teachers in both the United States and China. The authors would like to express their thanks to Gail Burrell (Michigan State University), who generously contributed funds toward this activity through NSF grant 0714890.

This workshop summary has been prepared by the workshop rapporteurs as a factual summary of the main presentations and discussion at the July 2009 workshop. Chapters 1 and 2 provide background on the educational systems in China and the United States, respectively, particularly as that background affects the preparation and practices of mathematics teachers. Chapter 3 describes the preparation and roles of mathematics master teachers in China, while Chapter 4 covers similar topics in the United States. A final chapter presents key questions identified by speakers at the workshop that remain to be answered. The statements made in this summary are those of the rapporteurs or individual workshop participants and do not necessarily represent the views of all workshop participants, the USNC/MI, or the National Academies.

This report has been reviewed in draft form by individuals chosen for their diverse perspectives and technical expertise, in accordance with procedures approved by the National Academies' Report Review Committee. The purpose of this independent review is to provide candid and critical comments that will assist the institution in making its published report as sound as possible and to ensure that the report meets institutional standards for quality and objectivity. The review comments and draft manuscript remain confidential to protect the integrity of the process.

We wish to thank the following individuals for their review of this report: Jinfa Cai, University of Delaware; Roger Howe, Yale University; Cathy Kessel, consultant; James Lewis, University of Nebraska, Lincoln; Xuhui Li, California State University, Long Beach; Edward Liu, Rutgers University; James Rubillo, DeSales University; and Tina Straley, Mathematical Association of America.

Although the reviewers listed above have provided many constructive comments and suggestions, they were not asked to endorse the content of the report, nor did they see the final draft before its release. Responsibility for the final content of this report rests entirely with the authors and the institution.

Ana Ferreras and Steve Olson, *Rapporteurs*

Contents

FIGURES

BOXES

1

Comparisons Between Mathematics Education in China and the United States

Liping Ma began the workshop with a general comparison of mathematics education in China and the United States. Ma taught elementary school for 7 years in China before earning a master's degree in teacher education at East China Normal University and a doctorate from Stanford University. Drawing on her knowledge and experience in both countries, she presented her assessment of similarities and differences in the two systems. This chapter summarizes her remarks as well as selected comments from others.

THE ORGANIZATION OF EDUCATION

Education in China is divided into 6 years of elementary school, 3 years of middle school, and 3 years of high school (high school is not compulsory), with the first 9 years being compulsory education. (See Box 1-1.) Admission to high school is by competitive exam, with about 50 percent of high schools offering general education and 50 percent offering vocational education. Parents provide support for their children to attend high schools, and scholarships are available for students from poorer families. School hours are from 8:00 a.m. until 5:15 p.m. for high schools (compared to approximately 7:30 a.m. to 2:15 p.m. for many U.S. high schools). Usually, one school in each city is designated to provide special education for students with disabilities. There is no home schooling in China, unlike in the United States. There are few athletic and nonacademic extracurricular

BOX 1-1
China-U.S. K–12 Educational Levels Comparison

China	United States
Primary education and elementary school start at the age of 6 and last 6 years. Secondary education consists of 3 years of middle school and 3 years of high school. Mandatory education requires 9 years of education starting at the age of 6.	Primary education and elementary school consist of 5–6 years. Secondary education consists of 2–3 years for middle school and 4 years for high school. Mandatory education starting age and length varies by state.

activities. However, many students participate in after-school activities to prepare for tests, including the entrance exam to universities, which students can take just a single time (unlike the SAT Reasoning Test and ACT, which can be taken multiple times in the United States). Text messaging has become a popular way for teachers and administrators in China to communicate with parents about homework or school notices.

Many elementary school students learn mathematics from a specialized mathematics teacher, but that is not universal. In grades 1 and 2, the mathematics teacher may also teach Chinese literacy. In some places, mathematics teachers also teach science, though science is not a prominent part of the curriculum in Chinese elementary schools. In schools in rural or remote areas, an elementary teacher in China may teach all subjects, as is often the case in similar situations in the United States. Nevertheless, mathematics specialist teachers in elementary schools are common in China and less common in the United States.

BACKGROUND

Mathematics instruction in China using western notation[1] did not begin until 1894, when an American missionary, Calvin W. Mateer, published the first arithmetic book in Chinese that used Arabic numbers written horizontally rather than vertically. And mandatory elementary education was not instituted in China until 1904—52 years after the first mandatory school attendance law was passed in Massachusetts. However, Chinese culture has emphasized teaching and learning for thousands of years, Ma pointed out. At about the same time that Socrates (469–399 BC) lived in the West, Confucius (552–479 BC) was writing extensively about the role of teachers in society. (See Box 1-2, Confucius' Teachings on Education.) Confucius' teachings have remained a constant part of Chinese education, which has not been the case with Socrates.

Even today, Ma observed, all Chinese students learn several sayings from Confucius directed specifically toward education. These sayings can be summed up in three phrases:

To silently appreciate a truth.
To learn continually.
To teach other people unceasingly.

Confucius established a tradition of deep respect for teachers in China, which forms a component of what Ma called "the invisible part" of education. "We don't see it when we go into classrooms. But it is in teachers' minds." Even during the Cultural Revolution in China, when books were largely abandoned, ideas about teaching and learning were preserved in the culture.

Today, teachers in China are still highly respected. "Teachers at any level are respected by all people in society," mentioned Shiqi Li, a professor of mathematics education at East China Normal University. "Especially they are respected by students and their parents." The career hierarchy for Chinese K–12 teachers (described in Chapter 3) is comparable in prestige to that for higher education, and master teachers see themselves as being at the same level in the K–12 system as distinguished professors do at universities.

---

[1] The notation for numbers and algorithms used in the United States and Europe.

BOX 1-2
Confucius' Teachings on Education

In his teaching, the superior man guides his students but does not pull them along; he urges them to go forward and does not suppress them; he opens the way, but does not take them to the place. Guiding without pulling makes the process of learning gentle; urging without suppressing makes the process of learning easy; and opening the way without leading the students to the place makes them think for themselves. Now, if the process of learning is made gentle and easy and the students are encouraged to think for themselves, we may call the man a good teacher.

Only through education does one come to be dissatisfied with his own knowledge, and only through teaching others does one come to realize the uncomfortable inadequacy of his knowledge. Being dissatisfied with his own knowledge, one then realizes that the trouble lies with himself, and realizing the uncomfortable inadequacy of his knowledge, one then feels stimulated to improve himself. Therefore it is observed, "The processes of teaching and learning stimulate one another."

RESOURCES AND REWARDS FOR TEACHING

Ma explained that Chinese teachers have three kinds of intellectual resources for improving teaching: "wisdom of teaching passed down throughout history," regular exchanges among colleagues, and recent research on education. In contrast, the main intellectual resource for teachers in the United States is new ideas about education generated by educational research. Most U.S. teachers do not learn the theories directly, but they learn new approaches based on the theories, which they implement in their classrooms. Also, regular exchanges among teachers, which are common in China, are less frequent in U.S. elementary schools. In addition, teachers' self-reflection in China is an important way to improve teaching.

Ma described two kinds of rewards that motivate U.S. teachers. One is salary, and the second is personal interest in students. In her opinion, salary levels are not as important in China as in the United States: "Chinese teachers think, 'Okay, the salary is not bad.'" The U.S. system is more professional. In contrast, Chinese teachers have the "moral satisfaction" of being a teacher.

THE CONTEXT OF TEACHING

The physical layout of Chinese classrooms differs from that of U.S. schools (Figure 1-1). Chinese teachers have much larger classes: typically around twice the size of U.S. classes. When Ma was an elementary school teacher in China, she said, she had classrooms with as many as 60 students, and she has attended classes in China that have more than that. Also, classes in China typically have all of the desks facing the teacher, whereas in the United States, desks may be clustered into groups so that students can work together (though many U.S. classrooms are still organized along traditional lines, as in China). As a Chinese teacher, I don't feel comfortable if I don't see all the eyes of my students. When we teach math, we all focus on math. But in U.S. classrooms, many things are going on."

Also, in Chinese schools, students tend to stay in one room and teachers travel to that room to teach. In the United States, teachers can decorate and be creative in their homeroom, Ma explained, because they "own" the room. But in China, students own their rooms and teachers travel to them.

The home base for teachers in China is typically a teachers' room shared by several teachers. These rooms are primarily for work rather than for relaxation. They have desks, tables, a telephone, and bookshelves (Figure 1-2). Teachers use these rooms to grade homework, prepare and analyze les-

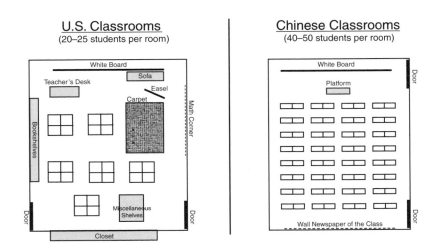

FIGURE 1-1 U.S. classrooms versus Chinese classrooms (Liping Ma).

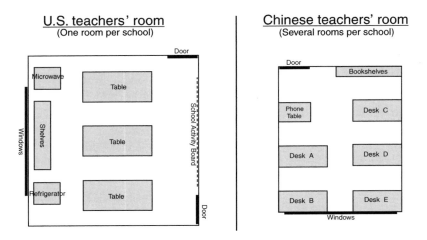

FIGURE 1-2 U.S. teachers' room versus Chinese teachers' room (Liping Ma).

sons, and interact with other teachers. Teachers' rooms often are for teachers of the same grade or same subject, so that they can work together.

In contrast, Ma observed that many teachers' rooms in the U.S. schools tend to be geared more toward relaxation than work. U.S. teachers spend less time in teachers' rooms and more in their homerooms compared to Chinese teachers. As a result, they are less likely to see their colleagues in teachers' rooms, reducing their opportunities to collaborate.

U.S. teachers' rooms are organized for both work and relaxation, whereas Chinese teachers' rooms are a base for work and collaboration throughout the school day.

Chinese teachers have fewer classes than do U.S. teachers, typically just two or three per day, whereas U.S. teachers are in their classrooms for most, if not all, of their day. (See Box 1-3, A Day in the Life of a Chinese Teacher.) Outside the classroom, Chinese teachers spend considerable time grading homework. "That way, they know what problems students are encountering in doing the homework," described Fang Wei, a teacher at Suzhou High School in Jiangsu Province. With 40 to 50 students per class, a teacher might have 90 homework assignments to correct each day. In Wei's school, the 28 mathematics teachers are separated into two teachers' rooms with facing desks so they can talk with each other as they are marking homework or preparing lessons. Teachers typically use a teachers' room to answer students' questions and help weak students. When a student is present, they mark his or her homework, so that the student can correct it in person. Chinese teachers may have an hour and a half for lunch, compared with 20 to 30 minutes for many teachers in the United States.

In China, teachers often sit in on lessons given by other teachers and provide the teachers with comments after the class. Master teachers also give demonstration lessons to all of the mathematics teachers in a school. Every week there is time for mathematics teachers to discuss teaching, either in a whole group or divided by grades. Common topics for discussion are reflections about lessons, getting help with trouble spots, making connections between content areas, getting across difficult points, analyzing student errors and solution methods, and sharing successful experiences. Sometimes, teachers also discuss mathematics education with mathematics teachers from other schools, education experts in universities, or master teachers from other cities. All of the mathematics teachers in the city of Suzhou, for example, have a specific time set aside on Thursday afternoons when they are not teaching so that they can meet to discuss mathematics education and see if they are progressing at the same pace. Hongyan Zhao, a master teacher in Beijing, estimated that mathematics teachers in China spend about one-third of their time while in school on lesson planning and preparation, one-third of their time teaching, and one-third of their time engaged in discussions with other teachers (including grading).

Testing in China is focused on the tests given at the end of middle school and high school that dictate entrance into high schools and colleges, respectively. In addition, at the local district or city level there is a universal final exam for mathematics given at the end of each academic year that is voluntary, though most schools participate. Testing, which has been used for thousands of years in China for government hiring, is viewed as less critical in China than in other countries such as the United States. The prevailing view is that if students work hard they all have the potential to do well on tests. An important factor in judging teachers has been the success of their students on high school and college entrance exams, but more recently and in the larger cities, other aspects of teacher performance are being assessed. For example, peer evaluations and student evaluations are becoming more important.

CHANGES IN CHINESE MATHEMATICS EDUCATION

Mathematics education in China has been undergoing important changes in recent years. Reform efforts patterned in part on the standards

---

BOX 1-3
A Day in the Life of a Chinese Teacher

Hongyan Zhao, a master teacher at the upper secondary school attached to Tsinghua University in Beijing, described a busy but not unusual day in her life as a teacher. She arrived at the school at 7:30 a.m. to begin work. First, she went over the lesson plan before going to class, reviewing the best way to teach her students about linear equations. She then taught a lesson to a class of grade 12 students, with the first part of the lesson being teacher-oriented, and the second part, student-oriented. "I raised the question of how many ways there were to express the linear equations, and the students would discuss it first, and then write down the result on the blackboard."

She then taught a lesson to grade 11 students, part of which involved letting them enclose various rectangles with rope. "When the conditions were simple, they could finish the tasks by using their knowledge of arithmetic. When the conditions were complicated, they could use their knowledge of equations to get the length and width of the rectangle to finish the tasks."

Next, she observed a class taught by a young teacher who had been teaching for 3 years. "The lesson was about geometric proof. I found that most students listened carefully, but I still found a few stu-

---

developed by the National Council of Teachers of Mathematics (NCTM) have sought to make mathematics instruction more effective for all students. For example, Chinese classrooms traditionally have been organized in such a way that student discussion is difficult, but Chinese teachers have come to recognize that student discussions can benefit learning (for additional information on Chinese student learning, see Cai and Cifarelli, 2004). As a result, Chinese teachers have begun to encourage students to participate in discussions, even though their classrooms are not set up for such discussions.

dents had difficulties following the teacher. I exchanged opinions with the teacher after class and showed him another proof and talked with him on how to improve the effectiveness of the lecture in class."

After that, she graded students' homework and corrected tests from the previous day. "I found that they still had some problems understanding the knowledge of functions. I talked with those who had more difficulties with it." She also gave three advanced students an assignment to do research on several questions that had recently appeared on the National College Entrance Exams.

Next, she attended a group activity to prepare lessons, part of which was devoted to helping one of the younger teachers learn how to give students individual help based on their level of understanding. She then attended a lesson-preparing activity in the nearby lower secondary school. "Master teachers must attend such activities, giving advice on the arrangement of the teaching program and the transition of knowledge between junior and senior high schools."

Finally, she attended a meeting in her school, where she gave two assignments to fellow teachers. One was to ask each teacher to write a summary of the work done in the previous semester. The other was to write the work plan for the next semester.

"This is one of my workdays, busy but fruitful."

At the same time, the focus on student achievement remains very high in Chinese mathematics classrooms. Ma expressed the opinion that in the United States, teachers want to make their students happy in the present. But in eastern countries, teachers want their students to be happy in the future, which means that they need to work hard in school.

2

Mathematics Education in the United States

The United States is a large and diverse country with considerable variation across regions, districts, and schools. Edward Liu of Rutgers University's Graduate School of Education provided a general overview of teaching in the United States, with the caveat that descriptions may not be accurate in a given state or city.

THE HISTORY AND CONTEXT OF TEACHING

Teaching is honored in the United States, Liu said, "but in American culture it's also somehow looked down upon. If you mention that you are a high school teacher, someone will often respond, 'That's terrific,' but the next sentence out of their mouth is, 'You must like the summer vacations off.' So it gets a mixture of some respect and some lack of respect." Teaching is seen as a profession in the United States, but it is a relatively low paid one and is unionized, which many other professions are not.

The U.S. education system is decentralized and fragmented. Preparation and credentialing, working conditions, and job definitions are set at the state and local levels. And there are approximately 14,500 school districts in the United States with elected local school boards that make policy.

The United States does not have a national curriculum, and because of local control, schools can undergo frequent policy or curricular changes. "You can be a veteran with lots of expertise in a math curriculum," Liu commented. "Suddenly a new school board comes in and changes the curriculum or approach, and then this is all new to you. What you have learned and the lessons you have designed may no longer be as valuable or as useful. That can be very disruptive."

The cultural context also has an influence on teaching and learning. In the United States, teaching tends to be associated with individualistic, heroic images. "Successful teachers are charismatic, they have personalities, they are dedicated; on their own they are inspiring students. If you look at a movie, you never see teachers working together or talking to one another. They're all with their students being inspirational."

The teaching profession itself has a culture that emphasizes autonomy and privacy. "You are the king or queen of your classroom," described Liu. "You have a right to organize it as you feel to fit your strengths and weaknesses." The teaching profession traditionally has resisted outside intervention from administrators and the state, though that tradition is slowly changing.

Teaching also has a culture of egalitarianism that resists distinctions based on expertise and merit. "We all are the same and have equal status, equal pay, equal say, and equal rights to teach the way we prefer." In addition, teaching has a culture of seniority. When distinctions are made between teachers, those distinctions are usually tied to seniority rather than other criteria.

These cultural aspects of teaching have kept the profession relatively unstratified in the United States. There is little differentiation in job descriptions or pay. To gain increased responsibility and salary, teachers traditionally have had to leave the classroom and go into administration, although there have been some roles, such as department chair, that have a history of permitting teachers to stay in the classroom and take advantage of their instructional expertise.

Early career teachers have limited opportunities for apprenticeships and few entry procedures, Liu explained. New teachers are expected to start on their first day and be ready to teach a full load. "In fact, sometimes they get the most challenging course assignments, the lowest tracked students, and multiple assignments rather than the easier ones you would think would be given to a novice." This aspect of teaching also has been undergoing gradual change in some places as professional development programs and teacher residency programs have sought to provide a more gradual and graded entry into the profession and a longer-term novice experience.

THE PREPARATION AND PROFESSIONAL DEVELOPMENT OF TEACHERS

Teachers need to be well prepared if they are to teach mathematics well. Yet, according to Maria Tatto of Michigan State University's College of Education, the education of prospective teachers and the professional development of practicing teachers often do not provide the kinds of opportunities to learn that teachers need to be effective. "We are constantly asking teachers to teach things we have not prepared them for, and we are cheating our students of a good mathematics education."

Tatto is the principal investigator for an international comparison of educational policy known as the first Teacher Education Study in Mathematics (TEDS-M).[1] TEDS-M has just finished a systematic study of preservice mathematics preparation in 17 countries, including the United States. The study looked at prospective K–12 teachers' characteristics and opportunities to learn, the outcomes of these opportunities, and the impact of these opportunities on novice and experienced teachers. It had three components:

1. Studies of teacher education policy, schooling, and social contexts at the national level

2. Studies of primary and lower secondary mathematics teacher education routes, institutions, programs, standards, and expectations for teacher learning

3. Studies of the mathematics and related teaching knowledge of future primary and lower secondary school mathematics teachers

Data collection for the study began in October 2007 and ended in June 2008. It surveyed more than 15,000 future primary teachers, more than 9,000 future lower secondary teachers, more than 4,000 teacher educators, and about 500 institutions that included units preparing future primary and lower secondary teachers. In addition to measuring background, opportunities to learn, and beliefs among teachers in each country, the study included items measuring teachers' mathematical content and pedagogical knowledge. "We did not originally intend to test teachers, but the countries said, 'If we're going to do all this work, let's develop a good test.' And that was a good thing to do," commented Tatto.

The results of the study were planned for release in January 2010 and

---

[1] For more information on TEDS-M, see http://teds.educ.msu.edu.

were not available at the time of the workshop. The study also planned to release a large database of results in September 2010 for use by researchers and others.

The literature review done for the study showed that teacher education, recruitment, and pay are highly decentralized in the United States, Tatto reported. All states require certified teachers to have completed a bachelor's degree that includes subject matter and pedagogical studies for an initial credential. Many states have additional requirements for further certification, such as additional courses or a master's degree. But other requirements for teacher certification vary by state. Some states have provisions for alternative or emergency certification that allow people who have not met all the state requirements to teach, usually on a temporary basis.

Teacher education is provided by a wide range of organizations, including colleges, universities, school districts, state agencies, and private organizations, Tatto explained. For example, more than 1,300 colleges and universities offer teacher preparation programs in early elementary, elementary, middle, and lower secondary education. Degrees offered include bachelor's degrees, master's and other postbaccalaureate degrees, and 5-year degrees.

As of 2007, 39 of the 50 states required 5 to 18 weeks of student teaching. These preparation programs vary widely in such factors as oversight of the selection of the cooperating teacher, the amount of contact between program faculty and field supervisors, and the links between coursework and field experience. In 2003, about one in five public school teachers was newly hired. Many alternative routes to teacher certification have been established during the past 20 years. For example, many large urban areas have approved alternative licensure programs for midcareer professionals seeking entry into teaching, and the federal government sponsors a program called Troops to Teachers to facilitate entry of former military personnel into teaching. These programs typically enable teaching candidates to begin working as full-time teachers while they meet the licensing requirements for standard teaching licenses.

TEDS-M also assessed the quality of the pool of teacher candidates using their SAT scores as a proxy. Future teachers who pursue elementary education with certification in mathematics tend to have lower SAT scores than the average college graduate. Teaching candidates who pursue secondary education licensure in specific subject content areas such as mathematics have average or higher SAT scores than other college graduates.

A fact-finding study for TEDS-M measured teachers' content and pedagogical knowledge as a trial run for the assessment used in the full study. Future teachers in the United States scored lower on most measures of mathematics content knowledge than did teachers from Bulgaria, Germany, Korea, Mexico, and Taiwan. "In the different areas of knowledge that we measured," Tatto explained, "the United States is pretty low." She cautioned, however, that these results are preliminary and do not include a representative sample of teachers from each country.

WHAT MATHEMATICS TEACHERS NEED TO KNOW

Comments from several of the other presenters echoed the findings offered by Tatto. Mari Muri, a senior mathematics consultant for the Project to Increase Mastery of Mathematics and Science at Wesleyan University, noted that most elementary teachers in the United States are trained as generalists and do not have much mathematics training. In most states they have taken 6 credit hours of mathematics, with that number rising to 12 credit hours in some states. "There's not a lot of math there," observed Muri, "and many are very uncomfortable teaching mathematics."

Muri laid out some of the knowledge and skills that elementary teachers need to teach mathematics well. They need to have a solid grounding in mathematics and believe that mathematics is important. They also need to have a thorough understanding of pedagogy. For example, they need to know how to teach children with different learning styles and backgrounds. "Students have different interests in mathematics and different parental support, so you need to have that passion for making sure that all of them can learn." Advanced students need to have their understanding of mathematics broadened rather than simply moving them to subjects covered in the next grade, while less advanced students need help to catch up with their peers.

To teach students with different learning styles, teachers need different ways of transmitting information. "If something doesn't work, just saying it louder or slower does not work," Muri commented. Teachers should explore innovative strategies such as taking students outside or on field trips, "or come dressed in some crazy outfit to motivate them." Teachers also need to be adept at teaching students who do not speak English at home. Many states such as California already have high numbers of English language learners in classrooms, and the numbers are growing throughout the United States.

Teachers need to have a solid understanding of how to assess students and how to use that information to adjust instruction. Furthermore, assessment is closely related to the communication of mathematics, Muri commented. "Promoting discussion in the classroom starts from an early grade, so that students are comfortable talking about mathematics and use proper mathematical terms and language." The teacher then can use students' verbal reflection on mathematics as formative assessments to improve instruction.

Teachers need to be able to use technology in mathematics instruction. Many new technologies are becoming available, "but that's something that most teachers at the elementary level are not really comfortable with," Muri described. "We need to make sure that they have that level of comfort."

The professional development of teachers differs in important respects from teaching students. "Adult learners are not children," she mentioned, "we need to treat them as adults." Elementary teachers may resist learning mathematics, as may administrators. Professional development "needs to choose instruction to motivate even the teachers who come in having no mathematics background or no love of math, who are walking in the door and out almost at the same time."

U.S. teachers do not model lessons for other teachers nearly as much as Chinese teachers do, Muri noted. Chinese teachers "are more comfortable visiting each other's classrooms and observing a lesson." The structure of a teacher's day in the United States also does not permit easy collaboration. However, some districts have found ways to address this problem. For example, Javier González, a mathematics teacher at Pioneer High School in Whittier, California, noted that all of the students in his school leave at 2 p.m. on Mondays, giving teachers 1 hour to work together, and once a month they leave at 12:15, providing the teachers with 2 hours of collegial time.

However, simply providing teachers time for collaboration does not mean that they will be able to use all of that time solely to improve instruction. For example, Mary Santilli, a teacher and program leader for elementary mathematics in Trumbull, Connecticut, described some of the activities undertaken by the Connecticut Investigations Consortium, which works with prekindergarten through fifth grade teachers who use a curriculum known as "Investigations in Number, Data, and Space." The consortium helps teachers understand and use the resources provided with the curriculum. However, the teachers also have spent considerable time rearranging the curriculum so that the order of topics covered in their classrooms matches up with the state assessments in mathematics. "Because of our state tests, it doesn't always make sense to go in order. We had to do some rearranging, and there was passionate debate among our group to arrive at an end product."

CHANGING THE CULTURE OF TEACHING

"The culture of teaching has a profound effect on the day-to-day activities of teachers," commented Janine Remillard of the University of Pennsylvania's Graduate School of Education. She noted that U.S. education is in many ways based on a production model. "We often think about education like a factory, where we have inputs and get an output. The input is the untaught student, teaching happens in the system, and children learn as a result." That kind of model tends to emphasize efficiency, where production is maximized for a given input. It also tends to produce a disconnected workforce, where different people do different kinds of work. "It's a very horizontal model, where there isn't much vertical interconnection among the types of work people do."

This horizontal model of teaching can in turn contribute to a lack of trust in teachers, Remillard commented; "We don't put a lot of trust in the wisdom of teachers' practice. As a result, people outside of the work of practice, like researchers or professional developers, need to provide teachers with that wisdom." Echoing Liping Ma's comments, Remillard described this lack of trust as one of the unseen aspects of teaching. "That's something we struggle with in the United States," she mentioned. "We need to think about how to foster wisdom within practice."

Belinda Thompson, a National Board Certified Teacher with 9 years of experience teaching mathematics in grades 5 through 9, observed that attitudes vary within the United States. She described growing up in rural Kentucky, where the public schools were one of the largest employers and being a teacher meant that you were a college graduate. "In lots of rural areas and small towns, there is a different perspective on a teacher and how the community looks at a teacher."

However, González reiterated Remillard's observation about the lack of respect accorded to teachers. When he has visited other countries, he has been struck by the respect he received as a teacher. "In Japan, I was treated with such respect and honor, because I was a visiting teacher from the state of California.... When I go to Mexico and tell them I am a teacher, I am highly respected throughout that country, because I am a *profesor*. Yet in this country, for whatever reason, the teacher is not highly respected. Therefore, it is difficult for us to produce young students who say, 'When I grow up, I want to be a teacher.' They want to be doctors, lawyers, other things."

Demographic changes going on within the teaching profession may have an influence on the culture, mentioned Liu. A large group of teachers who entered the profession in the early 1970s are now retiring. "We have a large group coming in who can perhaps be reshaped by new policies. There is more interest in collaboration, and somewhat less concern about privacy. In fact, many of the new teachers I have interviewed say, 'Yes, I wish I had more feedback; I wish more master teachers would come to my classroom.' So this is a new generation with different expectations." In addition, many midcareer professionals are entering teaching with work experiences and skills and life experiences from outside education. "They potentially can put some pressure on the existing system to create change."

Jennifer Bay-Williams of the University of Louisville, who is past-president of the Association of Mathematics Teacher Educators, also pointed to the forces of change swirling around teaching. As evidence for a renewed focus on teaching in the United States, she cited several innovative proposals made by prominent commentators, such as journalist Thomas Friedman's call to eliminate federal income taxes for all public teachers, Secretary of Education Arne Duncan's call to pay more to teachers in high-needs subjects like science and mathematics, and writer Malcolm Gladwell's call for an apprenticeship system that allows candidate teachers to be rigorously evaluated. "Our country is putting a lot of effort and energy into thinking differently about teaching," Bay-Williams commented.

3

Teacher Preparation and the Roles of Master Teachers in China

Teachers and teacher educators with experience in three different parts of China described the progression that teachers follow as they rise through the ranks of their profession. Though the details vary from one region to another, the overall process is roughly consistent throughout the country.

THE PREPARATION OF TEACHERS

Future mathematics teachers in China are prepared through a variety of routes, according to Yeping Li of Texas A&M University. The minimum preparation required to be an elementary school teacher is the completion of a 3-year program of study at a normal school focused specifically on the preparation of teachers. Normal schools in China can admit middle school graduates, and the graduates of these normal schools can go on to teach elementary school. Teaching positions at the middle school and high school level typically require 4-year bachelor's degrees.

In recent years, the levels of academic preparation for Chinese elementary school teachers—traditionally lower than for U.S. elementary school teachers—have been increasing. Many prospective elementary school teachers have attended normal colleges that admit middle school graduates for 5-year teacher preparation programs or high school graduates for 3-year programs. In addition, normal or comprehensive universities offer 4-year bachelor's degrees for future teachers in middle and high schools, and these programs have been rapidly expanding.

Most future mathematics teachers major in mathematics in college, according to Fang Wei, a teacher at Suzhou High School in Jiangsu Province. If a teacher does not major in mathematics at a normal college, he or she must pass an examination to receive the necessary certification to teach. Students study both mathematical content and pedagogy, though Chinese colleges tend to emphasize content more than pedagogy for future teachers.

Prospective teachers engage in practice teaching during their preparation. Then, once they begin working, apprentice teachers are supervised by mentors appointed by the school and they prepare lessons with their mentors, according to Hua Huang, a teaching researcher at the Shanghai Municipal Education Commission. The apprentice observes the mentor's lessons, and the mentor reviews the apprentice's lesson plans, observes the apprentice's lessons, and gives immediate feedback.

PROGRESSING THROUGH THE CAREER HIERARCHY

Following their apprenticeship, teachers in China move through a clear career hierarchy. They begin at a second-rank level and then can move to first rank, to senior rank, and to a variety of "super" ranks. Teachers at more advanced levels teach the more advanced classes, including the final-year courses. Senior-rank teachers also have more opportunities to demonstrate lessons and to be part of exchange programs within a school system.

Teachers must meet specific criteria to move from one rank to the next, although criteria may vary from region to region. For example, to move from second rank to first rank in Jiangsu Province, teachers need to provide 1 year of lesson plans and be certified in English and computer literacy. They also need to complete 30 hours of continuing education. An additional 75 hours of continuing education are necessary to move from first rank to senior rank. To advance, the school recommends a teacher, and the teacher undergoes an external review process by experts in the teaching profession.

To reach higher ranks of teaching in China, teachers need to conduct research and publish their findings in scholarly journals.[1] Typically, this

---

[1] These journals in mathematics are similar to teaching journals such as *Teaching Children Mathematics, Mathematics Teaching in Middle School,* and *Mathematics Teachers in the United States.*

research is more practically than theoretically oriented. It might involve analyzing a lesson, discussing students' mistakes with a particular concept, or describing an innovative way of conveying an idea.

Advancing in rank often requires that teachers participate in teaching contests. These contests may be organized by governments at various levels or by education associations. Participants have tryouts in each school and then, at the district level, teach in front of a special evaluation panel. Teachers are judged on such factors as their mathematical accuracy, their instructional coherence, their interaction with students, whether the objectives of the lesson were accomplished, their use of technology, and their expressiveness and charisma. In some cases, they teach in front of their own students; in others, they draw classes at random. Typically, districts choose just a handful of people to progress to contests at the municipal or provincial level.

BECOMING A SUPERRANK TEACHER

Above the level of senior rank, the designation as a superrank teacher (*Te Ji Jiao Shi* in Chinese) recognizes the professional expertise of the individual. Superrank teachers "represent the honor and professional expertise of the recipient," mentioned Huang. "They are models for other teachers, expert in teaching, and have great reputations and accomplishments in mathematics education."

According to Jianxin Qi, director of the Suzhou Research Institute for Education Science, a superrank teacher must have "a distinctive personal style in classroom teaching." In their instruction, they must exemplify "practicality, innovation, flexibility, and teaching as an art." Superrank teachers are expected to develop their own ideas about teaching materials, classroom teaching, and teaching strategies. They should have a systematic understanding of mathematics, know how to integrate mathematics education and psychology into classroom teaching, and pay attention to mathematics as a culture. They need to be able to analyze textbooks with deep understanding; focus on important points, difficult points, and key steps during teaching; use students' mistakes and misconceptions as teaching points; assess students' learning progress; change teaching methods based on student learning; and reflect on their teaching practice as researchers.

To develop this level of expertise, they need to interact with other teachers, researchers, and other experts and share what they have learned. They also need to reflect on their own practice from the perspective of theory and challenges in the classroom. They need to find and bridge gaps between existing ideas and innovative ones and between innovative design and implementation. Teachers should "pursue perfection," commented Qi. They should take every new day as a new starting point.

The numbers of superrank teachers are very low. The city of Shanghai selects just 12 mathematics teachers every 3 years as superrank teachers for all of its schools, representing less than 1 percent of mathematics teachers. The evaluation process for these teachers is very strict. They are observed by other teachers and independent judges as they teach classes. They also discuss their lessons and teaching with other highly ranked teachers. Typically, they have published extensively in the research literature, and they are often the recipients of various teaching awards and honors.

In contrast to second-rank, first-rank, and senior-rank teachers, which are nationwide designations, the titles and responsibilities of superrank teachers vary by province or city. Thus, if a teacher moves from one province to another, he or she must apply to be a superrank teacher in his or her new jurisdiction.

Highly ranked teachers may have a variety of responsibilities. They may check the lesson plans written by new teachers or teachers who have been identified as ineffective teachers by students and parents. They typically do research and publish articles. They help other teachers understand mathematical concepts, the objectives of lessons, difficulties in teaching a given lesson, or the most effective way to teach a lesson.

In the past, most superrank teachers did not reach that level until they were in their 40s or 50s, according to Shiqi Li from East China Normal University. More recently, some teachers have been reaching these levels in their 30s. In response, some jurisdictions have established even higher levels of recognition so that teachers continue to have goals toward which to aspire. As Li mentioned, "Such a mechanism may push more and more master teachers to devote their effort to do their best work."

For example, the highest honor in teaching in Jiangsu Province is full professor rank. Such teachers need to demonstrate outstanding teaching, publish articles in provincial-level and national-level academic journals,[2] and earn a first-level prize in a provincial or municipal open teaching contest. Teachers apply for professor-rank status, are recommended by their

---

[2]For discussion of the distinction between provincial-level and national-level academic journals, see Cai, J., and B. Nie. 2007. Problem Solving in Chinese Mathematics Education: Research and Practices. *Zentralblatt fuer Didaktik der Mathematik (International Journal on Mathematics Education),* 39, 459–475.

schools, and then are reviewed by experts. These are similar to the steps taken in higher education institutions in moving from assistant professor to associate professor to full professor.

There were 28 mathematics teachers who were made full professor or superrank teachers in Jiangsu Province in 2006, according to Jiansheng Bao of East China Normal University. These teachers were responsible for:

- demonstrating a deep theoretical and content knowledge about their teaching area,
- demonstrating strong teaching abilities and rich experience in their teaching,
- demonstrating abilities to reform teaching methods creatively and lead local teaching and research activities,
- knowing newly developed ideas in teaching around the world and demonstrating highly creative teaching ideas and research abilities,
- demonstrating abilities to use modern information technologies in their classroom, and
- demonstrating high-level professional and moral responsibilities.

THE PROFESSIONAL DEVELOPMENT HIERARCHY

Besides the career hierarchy designated by ranks, China has a parallel hierarchy organized around professional development. The professional development of teachers is meant to be a life-long learning system, with communities of teachers organized into groups. Teachers generally participate in research groups in their schools or districts. These activities encompass the training of new teachers, professional training, the training of master teachers, and degree program study.

For example, in Jiangsu Province, teachers progress from provincial-, district-, or city-level master teachers to teacher leaders to excellent teachers, with each new designation involving additional responsibility for the professional development of other teachers. These teachers might organize activities to improve classroom management, do research on student abilities, or discover and disseminate the best practices among teachers in the city. "Professional development of teachers needs to be rewarded, just as students need encouragement," commented Qi.

The professional development structure is different from, but overlaps with, the ranking system. In Beijing, for example, there are three levels of professional development expertise, according to Jianming Wang of the

Beijing Institute of Education. The first is master teacher at the municipal level, the second is leading teacher at the municipal or district level, and the third is superrank teacher. Elevation of teachers to these positions is approved by the Beijing Commission of Education. Master and leading teachers are selected every 3 years for 3-year terms, after which time they have to be reselected. Only 2 percent of teachers fall into the master teacher category, so there are fewer than 2,000 among all K–12 teachers in Beijing. In mathematics, there are only about 140 master teachers in all of Beijing. The designation of leading teachers is even more selective. In Beijing, there are only about 30 leading K–12 teachers in mathematics, mostly in high school. At the highest level in the professional development hierarchy, there are only about 150 K–12 superrank teachers in all subjects in Beijing. The superrank title lasts a lifetime, so a teacher needs to retire for someone else to be named.

In Shanghai, levels in the professional development hierarchy are known as city-level and district-level teaching researchers. The individuals in these positions might play the role of a coach to teachers, demonstrate exemplary practices, do research on teaching, and conduct open lessons. Every school has a teaching research group, and there are research offices at the city and district levels as well. The system combines the training of teachers and research on teaching through a long-term and gradual process of professional development.

4

Teacher Preparation and the Roles of Master Teachers in the United States

In China, teachers advance along a clear professional hierarchy over the course of their careers. No such clear hierarchy exists in the United States. Presenters at the workshop commented that U.S. teachers' careers should instead be viewed as following "trajectories," with different routes possible at different stages of a career. Some of these routes lead toward positions that could be grouped under the heading of "master teacher," but these roles are extremely varied.

TRAINING AND CERTIFICATION

The one part of teachers' careers that does follow an established hierarchy, at least within each state or district, is initial certification, observed Yeping Li of Texas A&M University. Before certification, a teacher can be an assistant or student teacher. Assistant or temporary teachers also can be hired by schools to assist in classroom instruction. In addition, many districts have emergency certification processes that enable them to hire teachers who have not yet met the full certification requirements, e.g., Alternative Route to Teaching Certification.

Li used the state of Texas as an example of the certification process, while noting that the process varies in other locations. To obtain a teacher's certificate in Texas, a prospective teacher must complete a bachelor's degree in an academic major, complete a teacher training program, and pass the appropriate teacher certification tests. The first two requirements may be combined in the same program.

Colleges of education in Texas generally do not offer bachelor's degrees that include teacher training programs, but the Department of Teaching, Learning, and Culture, where Li works, does offer an interdisciplinary bachelor's degree that is acceptable for certification.

ADVANCED CERTIFICATION AND AWARDS

One way in which U.S. teachers gain enhanced recognition and responsibilities is through advanced certification. For example, the National Board for Professional Teaching Standards, which is a nongovernmental, nonprofit, and independent certification organization, has certified more than 70,000 teachers since the program began in 1987. In many states and districts, board certification triggers additional pay. Teachers also can earn greater pay and higher professional standing through graduate education and certification programs offered by educational institutions and other organizations.

In addition, teachers in the United States can earn a variety of honors and awards offered by government at various levels, colleges and universities, foundations, and private-sector organizations. For example, several presenters at the workshop had received the Presidential Award for Excellence in Mathematics Teaching. These kinds of honors and awards "help promote school education in this country," mentioned Li.

The criteria for these awards are not always clear or consistent, Li observed. Also, the achievements of the teachers who are honored do not necessarily paint a consistent picture of effective teaching.

As Jennifer Bay-Williams of the University of Louisville pointed out, many teachers remain classroom teachers for their entire careers. In general, pay rises with seniority and additional levels of education. An additional problem with both certification and awards, mentioned Bay-Williams, is that not many teachers strive for these exceptional levels of achievement. "It's not a systematic thing where everyone is trying and only a few get it," commented Bay-Williams. "We just have a few who are trying." Similarly, merit-based pay systems, in which teachers are rewarded on the basis of specific output, have been "largely unsuccessful" in the United States, she pointed out. "Many teachers don't like to be in competition, or on a career ladder, or having to put materials forth to show how good they are."

ADVANCED PROFESSIONAL ROLES FOR TEACHERS

There has been much interest in recent years in creating roles for teachers that incorporate specialized expertise and responsibilities, commented Edward Liu of Rutgers University. These roles can be extremely varied. They include math coaches and consultants, technology coordinators, mentor teachers, mentoring and induction coordinators, peer reviewers, special education inclusion coordinators, department chairs, grade-level team leaders, and house leaders.

The responsibilities assumed by these individuals are as varied as their titles. They may serve as informal resources to other teachers, open their classrooms to outside visitors, work with student teachers, interact with administrators, organize and deliver professional development, or oversee novice teachers.

The criteria that must be met to move into one of these roles are also varied. Possible factors are years of experience, leadership skills, extra credentials, and honors or awards. Typically, mathematics teachers in the United States start with their basic certificate and other credentials and then add other certifications, which may make them eligible to fill one of these roles. For example, seven states offer an advanced mathematics specialist certification, commented Bay-Williams. In contrast, she added, almost every state has roles identified specifically as reading specialists.

Despite their proliferation, many of these roles continue to be marked by challenges and limitations, Liu observed. Most teacher leadership roles are local and have not been formalized across jurisdictions. If extra pay is associated with these positions, the extra funding is often unstable and depends on the district or state budget. The job responsibilities and role descriptions are often unclear and vary from district to district and school to school, resulting in a lack of consistency. The criteria for selecting teacher leaders are often unclear, and among teachers there is some distrust about the criteria used for selection and the role of principals or other leaders in making decisions.

Finally, these roles sometimes clash with the existing professional norms of autonomy, seniority, and egalitarianism. This is especially true for roles involving educational reform or instructional leadership. "Once the role involves going into the classroom, observing other teachers, and offering critiques, teachers start worrying about their privacy," mentioned Liu. "The teachers who fill these positions can have difficulty trying to get the authority to implement their jobs, so they have to negotiate with other teachers to do their jobs effectively."

Another complication pointed out by several workshop participants is that master teachers may not be available where they are most needed. Some districts have sought to provide financial incentives for master teachers to work in high-need schools, but extra pay may not be enough to entice these teachers to change districts, especially since many mathematics and science teachers could receive higher salaries by working in the private sector. Retirement systems also can act as a barrier to movement, since teachers may lose part of their retirement benefits or seniority privileges if they move from one state or district to another.

Finally, becoming a master teacher often means that a teacher is no longer teaching in the classroom. "We rarely have a position that straddles teaching students and teaching teachers," commented Bay-Williams. "We take our best teachers and pull them out to have them help teachers, but then they are no longer teaching themselves, so they are no longer there as models in the classroom."

Mari Muri of Wesleyan University offered a different perspective on this issue. As a classroom teacher, she used to have influence on 24 students each year. "But if you can affect teachers who each have 24 students, it's a multiplier effect. I have to keep reminding myself of that."

RECEIVING AND PROVIDING
PROFESSIONAL DEVELOPMENT

One of the major responsibilities of master teachers is to provide teachers with professional development, and several presenters at the workshop spoke about the kinds of professional development that teachers need to become master teachers and that master teachers in turn should provide to other teachers. An effective teacher, commented Cindy Bryant, who was a mathematics teacher in Missouri for 25 years, not only knows mathematical content but also knows "the strategies to use, when to use them, and which to use with particular students." Effective teachers "focus on instructional strategies, have a repertoire of strategies to use, know how to manage their classrooms well, and [consider] what their students need to know."

In the opinion of Joann Barnett, a middle school mathematics teacher in Missouri, the professional development she received early in her career was not as useful as it could have been since she didn't know how to connect the activity to curriculum, instruction, and assessment. "Twenty-five years ago, the professional development provided to mathematics teachers in the United States was not very effective."

Encouraged by several positive professional development experiences, Barnett began searching for similar experiences, and soon she began offering professional development to the other teachers in her school. "School is not just a place for students to learn," mentioned Barnett. "Teachers learn, too, while they are at school. If our students see us excited about learning and if they see that we have a passion about teaching, our students are going to be excited about what they are learning."

Teachers need to know how to be effective with students at all levels of skill and academic achievement. "That's where instructional strategies really make a difference," commented Bryant. "Many times a student will not respond to one strategy, but if I try something else it might really grab that student." Teachers need to be able to ask questions appropriate to a situation, which requires profound content knowledge. They need to learn how to assess student learning and use that information to adjust instruction. They need to be able to use technology both for instruction and for data sharing and distribution.

Heather Callahan of the University of California, Los Angeles, also discussed the skills that master teachers need and how they can inculcate those skills in other teachers. Master teachers need to be able to develop teacher understanding of both mathematical content and pedagogy. In the United States, people tend to view mathematics as largely computational and fact driven. Therefore, "the first task of a master teacher is to help the teachers they are working with develop a balanced view of mathematics as a problem-solving and proving activity in which we use facts and computational techniques." Many teachers in the United States do not have enough background in mathematics to explain some of the concepts they teach, "which is perfectly understandable given our cultural understanding of the field of mathematics," mentioned Callahan. Master teachers need to help teachers develop a broad view of the mathematics they teach. "Teachers need to understand the big ideas of the content."

Master teachers also need to help teacher learners develop their pedagogical content knowledge, commented Callahan. Teachers should be able to employ numeric, geometric, and algebraic representations for students. They should employ a concrete-to-abstract pedagogy and inquiry-based activities. They should draw connections within the curriculum and be able to use modern technologies. They need to help teachers learn how to sequence tasks effectively and create and analyze assessments. Master teachers also need the ability to communicate their understandings effectively to other teachers. Two areas are especially important in this regard, according to Callahan. One is to facilitate teacher understanding through lesson modeling and analysis. The other is to engage teachers in examining student thinking.

Master teachers should help write instructional guides and curriculum charts, aid in assessment and interpretation of results, and provide teachers with opportunities to practice and to reflect on their teaching. As Callahan said, "A master teacher needs to be an effective communicator, listener, and facilitator of discussion among adults."

Callahan also said, "I don't enjoy it when someone stands in front of me and tells me what the theorem is." It is especially effective for teachers to learn new mathematics using the same methods they are being encouraged to use in their classrooms.

Master teachers acquire their expertise in many ways, observed Muri. Mathematics leadership institutes, such as those provided by the National Council of Supervisors of Mathematics, can provide valuable experiences. Universities are becoming more sensitive to the need of prospective and practicing elementary school teachers for courses not in calculus but in subjects that help them become better at the mathematics that they are teaching. Publishers and technology providers can be excellent providers of professional development. Muri mentioned the National Council of Teachers of Mathematics as an example of an organization that offers web-based seminars and courses as well as other web-based resources. "You're not going to go away [from any one experience] being a master teacher or mathematics specialist," she said. "But you sometimes gain the awareness, and that's the first spark. You become motivated to seek additional information."

CROSS-NATIONAL COMPARISONS

There are commonalities in effective professional development in China and the United States, highlighted Susan Nickerson of San Diego State University. Good professional development combines mathematical content with information on effective instructional strategies. It thrives on a passion for mathematics and asks for persistent endeavor. It relies on support from others with high academic standards, a vision of effective teaching, access to supplementary materials, and reflection on practice.

Chinese teachers have an opportunity to go much deeper in their professional development discussions, commented Nickerson, partly because they have more time for such activities and partly because the curriculum and policy environment in China tend to be more stable. Also, professional development tends to be much more individualistic in the United States, whereas in China it takes advantage of communities of practice.

Xue Han of the University of New Mexico agreed that professional development in China is systematic and organized, whereas in the United States it is more fragmented. "Based on my experience in the United States, many elementary school teachers do not have any professional development related to mathematics," she mentioned. In China, the professional development curriculum is closely tied to the mathematics curriculum and to the textbooks used in the class, while in the United States, professional development is often disconnected with what is taught in the classroom. "We offer a lot of snapshot workshops to teachers, or professional development is project-based. When the money is gone, the professional development is over. So there is no consistency across professional development experiences offered to teachers."

Despite the problems with professional development in the United States, differentiated roles, career ladders, induction programs, and more rigorous evaluation of teachers are "at the top of the federal, state, and local policy agendas," commented Liu. "Many different stakeholders are very interested in these issues, and there is lots of activity throughout the country."

BOX 4-1
Becoming a Certified Master Mathematics Teacher in Texas

Yeping Li described a process in the state of Texas that leads to certification as a Master Mathematics Teacher (MMT). To obtain the MMT certificate, a teacher must have at least 3 years of teaching experience, complete an approved MMT preparation program, and pass the MMT certification exam (which was first administered in June 2003). The responsibilities of an MMT involve teaching mathematics and mentoring other teachers, including working with other mathematics teachers or with content area teachers, depending on the needs of a particular school. MMTs who are designated by their districts to teach and mentor in high-need schools receive a year-end stipend from the state.

BOX 4-2
Summary of Key Differences in the Mathematics Teaching Profession in China and the United States as Identified by Workshop Speakers

CHINA

Math teachers are usually specialists even at the elementary level.

Teaching is a public practice with norms and structures that promote collaboration.

The teaching profession has a clear career hierarchy with distinct, formal ranks from novice (second rank) to master teacher.

Master teachers continue to teach and perform their additional responsibilities, using their classrooms as a base. Work occurs in the communal context of the school.

Professional development is embedded in the daily life of the school.

A national curriculum allows teachers more time for continuous improvement in lesson preparation.

K–12 teachers are actively involved in generating knowledge on how to improve teaching.

UNITED STATES

Math teachers are usually generalists at the elementary level and specialists at the secondary level.

Teaching is largely a private practice with norms and structures that favor autonomy.

The teaching profession does not have a clear hierarchy, though there is some movement toward creating differentiated roles for teachers.

Master teachers often have to move outside of the classroom to a new position, to take on additional responsibilities.

Professional development often occurs outside the daily life of the school.

Without a national curriculum, teachers often spend a lot of time aligning standards, curriculum, testing, and so on, rather than developing and reflecting on lessons.

There is a greater separation between research on improving teaching and actual practice.

5

Comparisons and Unanswered Questions

In the final session of the workshop, Susan Nickerson from San Diego State University and Shiqi Li from East China Normal University described several admirable aspects of each other's education systems and several aspects about the questions that remain.

THE U.S. PERSPECTIVE

Nickerson expressed admiration for the ways in which teachers are respected in China. "In the United States, we don't honor the teaching profession as we should," she commented. That is partly the responsibility of teachers and partly the responsibility of society. Parents appear to be more questioning of teachers and education in the United States, and they tend to act as consumers of educational services, which changes the relationship between teachers and parents.

Nickerson also praised the openness of teaching in China. When teachers present a lesson in public, the purpose appears to be both to help that teacher improve and to help other teachers improve. "In the teaching profession [in the United States], we still have a very isolated culture and are hesitant to have public practice."

The thoughtful and careful design of instruction in China was notable to the U.S. participants, especially the focus on lesson planning, key points, and points of difficulty. "A big part of our orientation is on designing the curriculum, whereas [Chinese teachers] focused on implementing the curriculum. In part, this is because China has a national curriculum, while we spend time aligning resources, so we don't have as much time to focus on implementation."

Finally, she highlighted the attention given to teacher research in China. "In China we see a very efficient system of integrating and aligning teaching and the study of teaching. There does not appear to be a separation between research and practice. Our impression is that Chinese teachers talk about teaching specifically, not generally, and about the practical aspects of teaching and not about teaching in a general sense. We feel that we have something to learn about that."

Nickerson mentioned that U.S. participants were curious to learn more about the ways in which teachers talk to each other, including how critiques are given and the level of analysis. They also wanted to learn more about the interactions of university professors with teachers. Many U.S. participants still had questions about the relative emphases on mathematical content and pedagogy in teacher preparation. And they wanted to know more about the use of both formative and summative assessments in China; for example, how do students perceive and prepare for the high-stakes tests that mark the end of middle school and end of high school?

THE CHINESE PERSPECTIVE

Li observed that Chinese participants were very impressed by the U.S. teachers who participated in the workshop, and especially by their ability to motivate students to learn through a wide variety of activities. There seems to be equality between teachers and students in the United States. In Chinese schools, many beginning teachers are very conservative and traditional.

Many Chinese participants expressed interest in the training and certification that U.S. teachers undergo. In China, commented Li, rankings are based on a teacher's daily performance, and "this evaluation system will be enhanced if we establish some kind of training system to identify and certify master teachers more rigorously and objectively."

Li expressed admiration for standards that have been developed in the United States in such areas as teaching effectiveness and assessment. Because these standards have been established through research, they are rigorous, he mentioned. The Chinese teachers also would like to learn more about teacher training at all levels. Case studies of teacher training would be especially interesting, including successes and problems that individual teachers have experienced.

Finally, the Chinese delegation was interested in learning more about the mathematical content of teacher preparation in the United States. In China, many teachers put content knowledge ahead of pedagogical knowledge, even though they know that the latter is also important. More information on teacher preparation and professional development in the United States could reveal the extent to which U.S. teachers are trained to deliver mathematical content effectively.

Future exchanges of educators from the two countries could help answer many of these questions, Li commented. In addition, analyzing teaching video clips or observing each other's classrooms in person could extend the learning process common in China today to schools in both countries. In particular, a library of videotapes of U.S. and Chinese mathematics classrooms, with translations and subtitles, would give U.S. and Chinese teachers opportunities to analyze and contrast lessons from both countries.[1]

---

[1]Arcavi, A., and A. Schoenfeld. 2008. Using the unfamiliar to problematize the familiar: The case of mathematics teacher in-service education, *Canadian Journal of Science, Mathematics and Technology Education* 8(3): 280–295.

References

RECENT RESEARCH ARTICLES ON EDUCATION IN CHINA

An, S. 2000. Globalization of education in China. *International Journal of Education Reform* 9:128–133.

An, S. 2008. Outsiders' view on Chinese mathematics education: A case study on U.S. teachers' experience in China. *Journal of Mathematics Education* 1:1–27.

An, S., G. Kulm, and Z. Wu. 2004. The pedagogical content knowledge of middle school mathematics teachers in China and the U.S. *Journal of Mathematics Teacher Education* 7:145–172.

Arcavi, A., and A. Schoenfeld. 2008. Using the unfamiliar to problematize the familiar: The case of mathematics teacher in-service education. *Canadian Journal of Science, Mathematics and Technology Education* 8(3):280–295.

Cai, J., and V. Cifarelli. 2004. Thinking mathematically by Chinese learners: A cross-national comparative perspective. In L. Fan, N-Y. Wong, J. Cai, and S. Li, eds., *How Chinese Learn Mathematics: Perspectives from Insiders*. Singapore: World Scientific Publishers.

Cai, J., and B. Nie. 2007. Problem solving in Chinese mathematics education: Research and practices. *Zentralblatt fuer Didaktik der Mathematik (International Journal on Mathematics Education)* 39:459–475.

Fang, Y., and L. Paine. 2000. Challenges and dilemmas in a period of reform: Preservice mathematics teacher education in Shanghai, China. *The Mathematics Educator* 5:32–67.

Li, Sh.-Q. 2006. Practice makes perfect: A key belief in China. In F. K. S. Leung, K. D. Graf, and F. J. Lopez-Real, eds., *Mathematics Education in Different Cultural Traditions: A Comparative Study of East Asia and the West*. New York: Springer.

National Research Council. 2003. Understanding Others, Educating Ourselves: Getting More from International Comparative Studies in Education. C. Chabbott and E. J. Elliott, eds. Committee on a Framework and Long-term Research Agenda for International Comparative Education Studies.

Li, Y., X. Chen, and G. Kulm. 2009. Mathematics teachers' practices and thinking in lesson plan development: A case of teaching fraction division. *ZDM-The International Journal on Mathematics Education* 41:717–731.

Li, Y., and J. Li. 2009. Mathematics classroom instruction excellence through the platform of teaching contests. *ZDM-The International Journal on Mathematics Education* 41:263–277.

Li, Y., D. Zhao, R. Huang, and Y. Ma. 2008. Mathematical preparation of elementary teachers in China: Changes and issues. *Journal of Mathematics Teacher Education* 11:417–430.

Li, Y. 2008. Mathematical preparation of elementary school teachers: Generalists versus content specialists. *School Science and Mathematics* 108:169–172.

Li, Y. 2008. Transforming curriculum from intended to implemented: What teachers need to do and what they learned in the United States and China. In Z. Usiskin and E. Willmore, eds., *Mathematics Curriculum in Pacific Rim Countries: China, Japan, Korea, and Singapore*, pp. 183–195. Charlotte, NC: Information Age Publishing.

Li, Y., Y. Ma, and J. Pang. 2008. Mathematical preparation of prospective elementary teachers. In P. Sullivan and T. Wood, eds., *International Handbook of Mathematics Teacher Education: Knowledge and Beliefs in Mathematics Reaching and Teaching Development*, pp. 37–62. Rotterdam, The Netherlands: Sense.

Liu, Y. 2008. Study of some aspects of mathematics teaching in secondary schools in China and England. *Journal of Mathematics Education* 1:40–48.

Paine, L. W., and Y. Fang. 2006. Reform as hybrid model of teaching and teacher development: Reforming teacher development in China. *International Journal of Educational Research* 45:279–289.

Paine, L., and Y. Fang. 2007. Supporting China's teachers: Challenges in reforming professional development. In E. Hannum and A. Park, eds., *Education and Reform in China*, pp. 173–190. Boston: Taylor and Francis.

Paine, L., and Y. Fang. 2007. Dilemmas in reforming China's teaching: Assuring "quality" in professional development. In M. T. Tatto, ed., *Reforming Teaching Globally*, pp. 21–53. Oxford, UK: Symposium Books.

Wang, J., and E. Lin. 2005. Comparative studies on U.S. and Chinese mathematics learning and the implications for standards-based mathematics teaching reform. *Educational Researcher* 34:3–13.

Wang, J., and L. W. Paine. 2001. Mentoring as assisted performance: A pair of Chinese teachers working together. *Elementary School Journal* 102:157–181.

Appendix A

The Teacher Development Continuum in the United States and China Workshop Agenda

Friday, July 31 – Sunday, August 2
Hyatt Regency Hotel
Newport Beach, California

United States National Commission on Mathematics Instruction
National Academy of Sciences
Sponsored by the National Science Foundation

PROGRAM NOTES

This workshop focuses on the teacher development continuum in the United States and China. We are particularly interested in how the professional lives of teachers are structured to receive ongoing professional development. We are also interested in how experienced and highly qualified teachers participate in this process as providers of professional development as master teachers, mentors, or coaches. These roles are titled differently within and across the two countries. We refer to these teachers in this program outline as "master teachers," even though that may not be their official title. One important focus for our discussions is comparing and contrasting the roles and status of master teachers in the two countries.

Opening Session – Friday, July 31, 2009

5:00 p.m. – 7:00 p.m.: Session 1 - Plaza III
Opening Remarks: Patrick Scott – USNC/MI Chair
Opening Speech: Liping Ma – Independent Scholar in the Field of Math Education
Chair and Moderator: Roger Howe – USNC/MI Planning Committee
Responder 1: Janine Remillard – USNC/MI Planning Committee

Responder 2: Shiqi Li – East China Normal University

Because of her unique circumstance in observing classrooms and talking to teachers in both countries, we have asked Liping Ma to share with us her impressions and perspective on two topics: the life of the mathematics teacher and the flavor of the mathematics classroom in the two countries. Two responders, one from the United States and one from China, have been asked to add their comments on these topics, after which there will be an open discussion on these topics.

Dinner: 7 p.m. – 8 p.m. - Plaza II

Saturday, August 1, 2009

7:45 a.m. – 8:45 a.m.: Breakfast - Garden

8:45 a.m. – 10:45 a.m.: Session 2 - Garden Room I
Glimpses into the Life of a Master Teacher – Videos of Master Teachers at Work
Chair and Moderator: Ann Lawrence and Janine Remillard
Presenter 1 (United States - Early Grades): Mary Santilli and Mari Muri
Presenter 2 (China - Early Grades): Fang Wei and Hongyan Zhao

We have asked four participants, two from China and two from the United States, to prepare 20-minute videos, each of which shows 6–10 short clips of what a master teacher does in a normal day. Two participants will present their videos today, one from each country, and the other two will present their videos tomorrow morning. Today's videos will focus on the early grades and tomorrow's will focus on the later grades. Each presenter will show his or her video in segments, giving a brief introduction to each segment, and will respond to questions or comments about the segment.

10:45 a.m. – 11:00 a.m.: Break - Garden

11:00 a.m. – 12:15 p.m. and 1:15 p.m. – 2:30 p.m.: Session 3 - Garden Room I
The Career Hierarchy in China and in the United States
Chair and Moderator: Joseph Rosenstein

Session 3a
Panelists: China
  1. *Jianxin Qi*
  2. *Hua Huang and Xue Bai*
  3. *Jianming Wang*

12:15 p.m. – 1:15 p.m.: Lunch - Garden

Session 3b
Panelists: United States
  1. *Edward Liu*
  2. *Jennifer Bay-Williams*
  3. *Yeping Li*

We have asked six participants, three from each country, to make 10-minute presentations about the career hierarchy in their country. The panelists will be university faculty who can provide perspective on what happens in the region in which their university is located; the teachers' perspectives will be the focus of Session 4. The panel on the career hierarchy in China will be before lunch (Session 3a), and the panel on the career hierarchy in the United States will be after lunch (Session 3b). After each group of three panelists have made their presentations, there will be time for questions and comments. Among the questions that we would like the panelists to address are the following:

• How is the career hierarchy structured in your region? How is this the same as, or different from, other regions?
• What are the ordinary ranks or categories of teachers?
  o How many are there? How are they distinguished from each other?
  o What are the duties of each rank?
  o Do teachers in these ranks interact in regular ways? Are there characteristic types of interactions between teachers in given ranks?
• What are the superranks or categories of teachers?
  o How many are there? How are they distinguished from the ordinary ranks and from each other?
  o What are the duties of the teachers in the superranks?
  o How do they interact with the teachers in the ordinary ranks and with each other?

- What are the criteria or conditions for promotion to the superranks?
     o Is there a progression in the superranks?
     o What percentage of teachers attain the superranks?
     o If there are different levels of superrank, what percentage at one rank graduate to the next one?

2:30 p.m. – 2:45 p.m.: Break - Garden

2:45 p.m. – 4:15 p.m. and 5:00 p.m. – 6:30 p.m.: Session 4 - Garden Room I
Becoming a Master Teacher
Chair and Moderator: Patrick Scott
Session 4a
Master Teachers: China
     1. Fang Wei
     2. Guoguang Zeng
Master Teachers: United States
     1. Cindy Bryant
     2. Joann Barnett

4:15 p.m. – 5:00 p.m.: Break - Garden

Session 4b
Master Teachers: China
     1. Jianxin Qi
     2. Jiansheng Bao
Master Teachers: United States
     1. Mari Muri
     2. Heather Calahan
Responder: Susan Nickerson

This session will also have two components. For the first component (Session 4a), we have asked four master teachers, two from each country, to discuss the career hierarchy from their perspective as master teachers. Among the questions that we would like the panelists to address are the following:

- How does someone become a master teacher?
- What is the status of teachers? What is the status of master teachers? Do teachers aspire to become master teachers?
- What is the normal progression through the ranks? How long is normally spent in each rank?
- What are the criteria or conditions for advancement?
- What is the portion of teachers in each rank at a given time?

For the second component (Session 4b), we have asked two master teachers (one from each country) and two university professors (one from each country) to discuss the preparation of master teachers focusing on two questions:

- What skills do master teachers need?
- How do they get these skills?

6:30 p.m.: Adjourn

Sunday, August 2, 2009

7:45 a.m. – 8:45 a.m.: Breakfast - Garden

8:45 a.m. – 10:15 a.m.: Session 5 - Garden Room I and Garden Room II
Small group discussions
Chair and Moderator: Joseph Rosenstein

The discussions will focus on issues raised on the previous day for which participants want further elaboration. In the initial 15–30 minutes, participants will suggest topics that they would like to discuss in smaller groups, after which we will break into about four groups of eight participants for 45-minute discussions, followed by reports from the small groups to the entire group.

10:30 a.m. – 12:15 p.m.: Session 6 - Garden Room I
Glimpses into the Life of a Master Teacher – Videos of Master Teachers
at Work (See description under Session 2.)
Chair and Moderator: Ann Lawrence and Janine Remillard
Presenter 1 (United States - Later Grades): Belinda Thompson and José Jarquin
Presenter 2 (China - Later Grades): Xue Bai and Guoguang Zeng

12:15 p.m. – 1:15 p.m.: Lunch - Garden

1:15 p.m. – 3:30 p.m.: Session 7 - Garden Room I
The Teacher Development Continuum
Chair and Moderator: Joseph Rosenstein
Presenters: China
 1. *Jiansheng Bao and Hua Huang*
 2. *Jianming Wang and Hongyan Zhao*
Presenters: United States
 1. *Maria Tatto*
 2. *Javier González*
Responder (United States and China): Xue Han

This session has two components: the first dealing with issues around the preparation of teachers, and the second with issues around the professional development of teachers. Each session will have two panelists, one from each country. Among the questions that the first group will address are the following:

- How does someone become a teacher of mathematics?
  - What college preparation is needed?
  - Is it different for elementary, middle, and high school teachers?
  - What mathematics courses are taken? What courses in pedagogy?
  - Is teaching in schools part of their preparation, and what does this consist of?
- How does a college graduate obtain a teaching position?
  - Is it based on examinations, interviews, recommendations, or performance in college courses?
  - Does the college graduate have to look for a position on his or her own?

- Who employs the teacher?
  - Is it a school, or a town, or a district, or a province?
  - Who is the teacher's "boss"?
  - Is the teacher in the civil service?
  - Do most teachers remain in the school in which they began teaching, or can they move from one school to another school?
- Who supervises the teacher?
  - Who decides whether the teacher's performance is acceptable and decides whether the teacher may continue teaching?
  - Does the teacher eventually have a permanent position, or is the teacher's position dependent on continued professional development?
  - How can a teacher lose his or her teaching position?

Among the questions that the second group will address are the following:

- How does training continue once a teacher has graduated from college and finds a position? What happens in the initial years?
  - Do they have reduced teaching loads?
  - Who provides training?
  - How much training is received?
  - Are they assigned mentors?
- What long-term mentoring and professional development does the teacher receive?
  - Are these programs voluntary or mandatory?
  - What opportunities are there for sharing and classroom visits?
  - When is the teacher considered to be "trained"?
- How is professional development structured?
  - Where does it take place? Is it in the school? Or is it at the university?
  - Are techniques like lesson study used?
  - Is there a culture of professional interaction?
  - What is the role of the master teacher in this professional development?
- How is professional development conducted?
  - Which forms does it take? One-to-one? One-to-many? Communal? In what portions?
  - Are there formal courses?
  - How does it mix content and pedagogy?

---

o Is professional development conducted by university staff or by master teachers? If both, would the two types work together or separately? If both, what portion is done by each?

o What professional development is conducted by other groups?

- How does professional development vary with rank?

o Is there a regular sequence of activities, or is it individually tailored, with wide variation?

o Does a teacher progress from receiving to providing professional development as he or she progresses in rank? Is this formalized, or is it simply a tendency?

3:30 p.m. – 3:45 p.m.: Break - Garden

3:45 p.m. – 5:00 p.m.: Session 8 - Garden Room I
Discussions and Closing Session
U.S. Chair: Janine Remillard
China Chair: Shiqi Li

During the first portion of this session, American and Chinese participants will meet separately to discuss:

- what they have learned thus far about the other country and how they might apply these lessons to their own country,
- whether their questions have been addressed and to formulate questions that are still unanswered, and
- what they would like to see as follow-up to the conference.

During the second portion of this session, each group will:

- describe what they have learned about the other country's practices,
- answer the other group's remaining questions, and
- present its ideas about follow-up.

There will then be a general closing discussion.

5:00 p.m.: Adjourn

Appendix B

Biographies of Workshop Participants

PARTICIPANTS FROM CHINA

Xue Bai graduated from Capital National University and worked as a teacher in Beijing No. 101 High School for 10 years. In 2003, Mr. Bai went to Haidian Teachers Training College and began to work as a teaching researcher.

Jiansheng Bao is a professor of mathematics education at the Department of Mathematics at East China Normal University. He was a high school mathematics teacher for about 6 years and earned his PhD in mathematics education at East China Normal University. His research interests include mathematics teacher education, psychology in mathematics education, and international comparisons in mathematics education.

Hua Huang is a senior teacher with a rich experience of 22 years in mathematics teaching. Currently, he is a teaching researcher at the Teaching Research Section of the Shanghai Municipal Education Commission. His responsibility is guiding mathematics teaching and mathematics teachers' professional development in the city. He is also a coauthor of a set of school mathematics textbooks for middle schools in Shanghai. His main research interests are school mathematics teaching and curriculum.

Shiqi Li is a professor of mathematics education at the Department of Mathematics and the deputy director of the Research Institute of Mathematics Education at East China Normal University. His research areas are mathematics learning, teaching, and teacher education. He is a coeditor of the book *How Chinese Learn Mathematics* (2004, World Scientific Publishing Co.). Professor Li has served as president of the China Association of Mathematics Education Research of Teacher Education Institutions.

Jianxin Qi is a *Te Ji Jiao Shi* and director of Suzhou Research Institute of Education Science. He has worked in several schools for more than 20 years. Mr. Qi is the recipient of numerous awards of excellence from the government of China, including the National Excellent Teacher Award in 1993, the Excellent Young Teacher in Jiangsu Province in 1995, and first-class Su Buqing Mathematics Education Award. He has published more than 100 research papers.

Jianming Wang is a professor of mathematics education and chair of the Department of Mathematics at Beijing Institute of Education. He also serves as vice board-chairman of the Beijing Mathematics Academy. Professor Wang has been responsible for designing the National Standards of High School mathematics of China, and training materials for teachers' training programs for all kinds of mathematics teachers.

Fang Wei received her BS degree in mathematics education at Soochow University. She has been teaching students aged 13–18 for 14 years and is a master mathematics teacher at Suzhou High School, Jiangsu Province. Ms. Wei has been trained as a mathematics bilingual teacher and works at Suzhou High School 'A' Level Centre.

Guoguang Zeng graduated from Beijing Normal University with a major in mathematics in 1993. He then served as a mathematics teacher in Kongjiang High School in Shanghai for 4 years. He went on to East China Normal University, and earned an MS degree in mathematics education in 2000. Mr. Zeng served as head of the Department of Mathematics at Kong Jiang High School, and he is a senior mathematics teacher and director of the division of teaching.

Hongyan Zhao received her BS degree in mathematics education at Hebei Normal University and an MS degree at the Capital Normal University.

She is a master teacher at the high school attached to Tsinghua University, which is among the best high schools in China. Ms. Zhao has been a math tutor in middle school for 18 years and is a master teacher in the field of mathematics in Beijing.

PARTICIPANTS FROM THE UNITED STATES

Shuhua An, a native of China, is an associate professor and the director of the Graduate Program in Mathematics Education at the College of Education, California State University, Long Beach. She has had teaching experience in mathematics and mathematics education at various levels for 24 years in both China and the United States. Dr. An is the author of the book entitled *The Middle Path in Math Instruction—Solutions for Improving Math Education.* Dr. An is a member of the editorial board of the *Journal of Mathematics Education* and an associate editor of the *Journal of the School of Science and Mathematics.*

Joann Barnett has been teaching middle school mathematics for 27 years. She has worked with various mathematical committees at the local, state, and national levels and is presently serving on the Program Committee for the 2011 National Council of Teachers of Mathematics (NCTM) Annual Meeting. She was the recipient of the 2003 Presidential Award for Excellence in Mathematics Teaching. She has been a master consultant with Missouri Math Academies for many years.

Jennifer Bay-Williams is the immediate past-president of the Association of Mathematics Teacher Educators (AMTE). She is associate professor and assistant chair in the Department of Teaching and Learning at the University of Louisville, Kentucky. She has been a leader in NCTM, including the writing and editing departments for *Mathematics Teaching in the Middle School.* Dr. Bay-Williams has published many articles, books, and book chapters focused on teachers. Dr. Bay-Williams received her PhD at the University of Missouri, Columbia.

Cindy Bryant served as mathematics teacher for 25 years in Missouri. She is the past president of the Missouri Council of Teachers of Mathematics, a past member of the NCTM Board of Directors, and a recipient of the 1996 Presidential Award for Excellence in Mathematics and Science Teaching. In addition, she served a 3-year term on the American Statistical Association and NCTM Joint Committee. She has been a master consultant for numerous Missouri Math Academies and currently serves as the mathematics curriculum consultant for the Missouri Department of Elementary and Secondary Education.

Peg Cagle teaches eighth grade honors algebra, honors geometry, and French at Lawrence Gifted/Highly Gifted Magnet school in the Los Angeles Unified School District (LAUSD). She has an MS degree in mathematics education from California State University, Northridge. She is National Board certified in Early Adolescent Mathematics. Ms. Cagle's honors include the Los Angeles City Teachers of Mathematics Association Excellence in the Classroom Award (2003), the Raytheon Math Hero Award (2006), the USA Today All-USA Teacher Team (2007), LAUSD Teacher of the Year (2008), and the Presidential Award for Excellence in Mathematics and Science Teaching.

Xiaoqing Chen is a doctoral candidate with the Department of Education at the University of California, Irvine. She was an English lecturer for 8 years at Xi'an Foreign Languages University, where she earned her BA in English language and literature, and MA in translation studies (Chinese to English/English to Chinese). Ms. Chen has translated at various international conferences while in China. She received a 5-month training in simultaneous interpretation at the European Union in Brussels in 2001.

Javier González is a mathematics teacher and department chair at Pioneer High School in Whittier, California. He is the creator of the Pioneer Math Academy, a 6-week summer math program that serves more than 700 students each year. He received the 1996 California Teachers of the Year Program award in mathematics, the Presidential Award for Excellence in Mathematics and Science Teaching, and the Milken Family Foundation Educator Award. He is a member of the National Academies Teacher Advisory Council and now serves as a member of the National Research Council's Mathematical Sciences Education Board and the California Teacher Advisory Council.

Xue Han, PhD, is an assistant professor in the Department of Teacher Education at the University of New Mexico. Her research focuses on elementary mathematics education and teacher professional development. She received her PhD in curriculum, teaching, and educational policy from Michigan State University.

José A. Jarquin has been the Title I coordinator at Charles R. Drew Middle School for the last 2 years. In May 2002, he graduated from California State University, Dominguez Hills, and began teaching at Drew Middle School as a sixth-grade math/science teacher. Mr. Jarquin's long-term goal is to open a school in his hometown in Oaxaca, Mexico.

Xuhui Li is an assistant professor in the Department of Mathematics and Statistics at California State University, Long Beach. He received his MS degree in mathematics from East China Normal University and his PhD in mathematics education from the University of Texas at Austin. Since 1992, he has engaged in secondary school mathematics teacher preparation and professional development activities as well as related research projects in Shanghai, Texas, Michigan, and California.

Yeping Li is associate professor of mathematics education at Texas A&M University. He is interested in examining issues related to mathematics curriculum and teacher education in various education systems and understanding how factors related to mathematics curriculum and teachers may come together in shaping effective classroom instruction. He has served as an associate editor for the *Journal of School Science and Mathematics*, and as a guest editor for the *International Journal of Educational Research and ZDM-The International Journal on Mathematics Education*.

Edward Liu is assistant professor of educational administration at Rutgers University, where he studies teacher hiring and retention, schools as organizations, leadership, and education policy. He has research affiliations with MetroMath: The Center for Mathematics in America's Cities, as well as with the Project on the Next Generation of Teachers at Harvard University. Dr. Liu is coauthor of *Finders and Keepers: Helping New Teachers Survive and Thrive in Our Schools* (published by Jossey-Bass) and has published in numerous scholarly journals.

Liping Ma is an independent scholar in the field of math education. Ma was senior scholar at the Carnegie Foundation for Advancement of Teaching during 2002–2008. She also served as a member of the National Mathematics Advisory Panel during 2005–2008.

Mari Muri serves as a senior mathematics consultant for the Project to Increase Mastery of Mathematics and Science at Wesleyan University in Connecticut. Before her retirement, she was a mathematics consultant at the Connecticut State Department of Education for 15 years. She taught at the elementary level and at the university level, preparing elementary teachers. She served on the NCTM Board of Directors, on the writing team for the NCTM Assessment Standards, as president of the Association of State Supervisors of Mathematics, and on the Mathematical Sciences Education Board.

Susan Nickerson is a faculty member of San Diego State University's Department of Mathematics and Statistics. Her research interest is in long-term professional development of elementary and middle school teachers. In particular, her focus is on describing, analyzing, and understanding effective contexts that promote teacher learning.

Mary Santilli is the program leader for Elementary Mathematics in Trumbull, Connecticut. Before teaching in Trumbull, Ms. Santilli worked as a primary teacher in Fairfield and Bridgeport, Connecticut. She is the cofounder of the Connecticut Investigations Consortium and has served on the executive board for the Associated Teachers of Mathematics in Connecticut (ATOMIC). Ms. Santilli has received the Presidential Award for Excellence in Mathematics and Science Teaching for elementary mathematics and the Christa McAuliffe Award for Excellence in Teacher Education. Ms. Santilli is also a PIMMS (Project to Increase Mastery of Mathematics and Science) fellow from Wesleyan University.

Joshua A. Taton is a second-year PhD candidate in teaching, learning, and curriculum at the University of Pennsylvania. In recent years, he has presented at several NCTM conferences on using technology in elementary and middle school laboratories and has written curriculum materials for a provider of e-Learning solutions in K–12 education. Before enrolling at the University of Pennsylvania, Mr. Taton taught middle- and high-school mathematics, while also coaching basketball and track and serving on technology-related committees. Mr. Taton holds a BA in mathematics from Yale University.

Maria Teresa Tatto is an associate professor at the College of Education in Michigan State University, where she has taught since 1987. Her research is characterized by the use of an international comparative framework to study educational reform and educational policy and their impact on schooling—particularly the role of teachers, teaching, and learning—within varied organizational, economic, political, and social contexts. Her work combines the use of quantitative and qualitative approaches and methods and provides a unique perspective on the study.

Belinda Thompson is a National Board Certified Teacher with 9 years of experience teaching mathematics in grades 5–9 in public and private schools in rural and suburban settings. She has also worked as a new teacher coach and teacher workgroup consultant in urban settings. She was a professional development designer and facilitator for two research projects funded by the Institute of Education Sciences (IES). Most recently she worked on two IES-funded research projects on teaching quality. She is a doctoral student at the University of California, Los Angeles, in the Graduate School of Education and Information Sciences.

PARTICIPANTS WHO ARE MEMBERS OF THE U.S. NATIONAL COMMISSION ON MATHEMATICS INSTRUCTION (USNC/MI)

Roger Howe earned his PhD in mathematics from the University of California, Berkeley, in 1969, and has been a professor of mathematics at Yale University since 1974. Dr. Howe has devoted substantial energy to issues of mathematics education, including serving on committees that have produced major reports on U.S. mathematics education since 2000. He is particularly interested in adapting the insights of other countries to improve mathematics education in the United States.

Myong-Hi (Nina) Kim is an associate professor of mathematics at State University of New York (SUNY), Old Westbury. Currently, Dr. Kim is working on the effect of computerized college mathematics at the proficiency level and has taken an instrumental role in improving the undergraduate program on mathematics teacher education at SUNY, Old Westbury. In addition, she was instrumental in the creation of a master's program for teacher preparation and enhancement, aimed at producing strong teachers. Dr. Kim earned her PhD in mathematics at the City University of New York in 1986.

Ann Lawrence has spent most of her mathematics teaching career in middle school, although she has taught in elementary and high school as well. Outside her classroom, she has worked as a math coach and in curriculum development at the school and district levels across the country. Ms. Lawrence has been an active member of the National Council of Teachers of Mathematics, including writing and reviewing journal articles and serving as a member and chair of the panel for the Mathematics Teaching in the Middle School. She has made numerous presentations at local, regional, and national NCTM conferences.

Janine Remillard is an associate professor of mathematics education and chair of the Foundations and Practices of Education Division of the Graduate School of Education at the University of Pennsylvania. Her research interests include mathematics teacher learning and change in urban classrooms, teachers' interactions with and use of mathematics curriculum materials, and the assumptions about the practice of teaching underlying curriculum development and implementation approaches. Dr. Remillard is coprincipal investigator of MetroMath, the Center for Mathematics in America's Cities, a Center for Learning and Teaching funded by the National Science Foundation. MetroMath is devoted to improving mathematics teaching and learning in urban communities.

Joseph G. Rosenstein has been a professor of mathematics at Rutgers University in New Brunswick, New Jersey, for the past 40 years and has focused on primary and secondary education for the last 20 years. He is the author of books and articles discussing discrete mathematics in the schools, and directs many professional development activities for primary and secondary teachers of mathematics. For the past 18 years, he has also served as director of the New Jersey Mathematics and Science Education Coalition, and has played key roles in developing New Jersey's mathematics standards. He is vice chair of the USNC/MI.

Patrick (Rick) Scott, chair of the USNC/MI, is the director of Pre-K through College (P–20) Policy and Programs at the New Mexico Higher Education Department. Dr. Scott retired in 2006 from New Mexico State University, where he had worked as a professor of bilingual mathematics education in the College of Education, to organize a new Math and Science Bureau in the New Mexico Public Education Department. He received a BS degree in mathematics from Stanford University, an MS in education from

California State University, Chico, and a PhD in mathematics education from Teachers College, Columbia University.

STAFF AND CONSULTANTS OF THE NATIONAL RESEARCH COUNCIL

Ana M. Ferreras is a program officer supporting the U.S. National Committees for mathematics, math instruction, crystallography, theoretical and applied mechanics, and physics. Dr. Ferreras holds a PhD in industrial engineering from the University of Central Florida (UCF). She also holds an MS in engineering management from the Florida Institute of Technology and a BS in electrical engineering from UCF. During her doctoral research, she assisted the Department of Industrial Engineering and Management Systems at UCF in reengineering the undergraduate curriculum by developing a national model, new programs, experiential laboratories, and research centers.

Kofi Kpikpitse is a program associate with the National Academy of Sciences. He manages the International Visitors Office and supports four U.S. National Committees within the National Academies. Mr. Kpikpitse has a BA in political science and a background in museum education.

Steve Olson has been a consultant writer for the National Academy of Sciences and National Research Council, the Howard Hughes Medical Institute, the National Institutes of Health, the Institute for Genomic Research, and many other organizations. He is the author of articles in the *Atlantic Monthly, Science, Smithsonian,* the *Washington Post,* the *HHMI Bulletin, Scientific American, Wired,* the *Yale Alumni Magazine,* the *Washingtonian, Slate, Teacher, Astronomy, Science 82-86,* and other magazines. From 1989 through 1992 he served as special assistant for communications in the White House Office of Science and Technology Policy. He earned a BS in physics from Yale University in 1978.

Ester Sztein is assistant director of the Board on International Scientific Organizations and supports the U.S. national committees for Quaternary research, geological sciences, geodesy and geophysics, and soil sciences. She pioneered the study of hormone metabolism in land plants within an evolutionary context and published her research in peer-reviewed journals. She collaborated as an editor with the Biometeorology Institute (Bologna, Italy) and worked on conservation and educational projects in Latin America and Africa. She taught plant biology at the University of Maryland and the University of Buenos Aires. She earned a PhD in Plant Biology from the University of Maryland and a BSc/MSc in Biology from the University of Buenos Aires, Argentina.